Original title:
Realm of Wonders

Copyright © 2024 Creative Arts Management OÜ
All rights reserved.

Author: Rosalie Bradford
ISBN HARDBACK: 978-9916-90-062-8
ISBN PAPERBACK: 978-9916-90-063-5

Mosaics of the Heart's Whisper

In silence, secrets softly weave,
Each shard a story we believe.
Colors blend in twilight's glow,
A tapestry of love we sow.

Fragments of laughter, pain, and grace,
Timeless moments we embrace.
In every piece, a pulse remains,
Whispers of joy, echoes of pains.

The Dance of the Wandering Spirits

Beneath the moon, they twirl and sway,
In twilight's grasp, they find their way.
Footsteps soft on midnight ground,
In gentle breezes, their songs resound.

Veils of mist, their cloaks of night,
Dance with shadows, slim and light.
Each turn a tale, each glide a dream,
In the silence, we hear their theme.

Flight of the Mirthful Soul

With wings of laughter, they take flight,
Soaring high in pure delight.
Clouds of joy, beneath them spread,
Where worries fade and hope is fed.

Colors bursting in the sky,
In every heartbeat, they reply.
The world beneath, a distant hum,
As mirthful spirits welcome fun.

Shadows Illuminated by Curiosities

In corners deep where shadows play,
Curiosities light the way.
A gentle spark in darkened lanes,
Reveals the beauty in our pains.

With open hearts, we start to see,
The wonders woven intricately.
Every mystery, a fleeting light,
Guiding us through the tranquil night.

Mirages of the Infinite

In the sands where shadows play,
Reflections waver, drift away.
Stars collide in whispered dreams,
Unraveling the fabric's seams.

Endless skies write stories bold,
Of secrets kept and tales untold.
In this vast, uncharted space,
We seek our truth, our destined place.

Waves of time gently unfold,
Visions bright, hearts of gold.
With every step into the light,
We find a spark that feels so right.

Through the mirage, clarity glows,
Binding threads only the heart knows.
We wander far, yet feel so near,
In the realms where dreams appear.

Whispers Beyond the Veil

Softly spoken, secrets pour,
Through the fabric, to the core.
Gentle echoes dance and swirl,
In the twilight, thoughts unfurl.

Voices linger, rich and low,
Guiding paths we yearn to know.
Faint and fleeting, shadows brush,
Stirring hearts in quiet hush.

Beyond the veil, the world aligns,
With every breath, new light defines.
Mysteries of the night unfold,
In the warmth, our hearts are bold.

As the whispers cradle dreams,
Life reveals its silver beams.
Through the dark, we shall prevail,
Hand in hand, beyond the veil.

Dreams in Celestial Gardens

Where starlit petals brush the sky,
Dreams take root and gently sigh.
In gardens lush, where time is still,
Whispers bloom on every hill.

Moonlit breezes weave a song,
Carried softly, sweet and strong.
Every flower holds a story,
Petals gleam with ancient glory.

Colors swirl in cosmic dance,
Awakening a timeless trance.
In this space, our spirits soar,
A tapestry forevermore.

Through the night, the heart does roam,
Finding peace in dreams' true home.
In celestial gardens vast and bright,
We harvest joy, our endless light.

Echoes from Enchanted Shores

Waves crash softly on the sand,
Whispers call from distant land.
Footprints left where ocean meets,
Carried far by rhythmic beats.

Every shell, a tale of old,
Secrets held, treasures told.
In the foam, the past unspools,
As sunlight paints the ocean's jewels.

The horizon blushes, bright and clear,
Echoes linger, drawing near.
In the twilight's gentle embrace,
We find solace, time and space.

Underneath the starry dome,
Hearts find refuge, wander home.
From enchanted shores, we hear,
The whispers of love, crystal clear.

The Bridge to Elsewhere

Upon a misty river's edge,
A bridge of dreams takes flight,
With every step, the past unwinds,
Leading hearts to new delight.

Beneath the stars, where shadows linger,
Whispers trace the evening air,
A path to worlds yet unexplored,
Where hope and wonder freely share.

Across the woods, the spirits call,
Their voices soft, a beckoning glow,
To step beyond the here and now,
To realms where wandering souls may go.

So take my hand, let us be brave,
In twilight's hush, our fears release,
For on this bridge, we rise and soar,
To find our peace, our sweet release.

Whimsy in the Forgotten Corners

In corners dim, where laughter hides,
A world of whimsy waits, unseen,
With teacups spun from dappled light,
And dreams that sparkle, soft and green.

Old shadows dance on cobbled streets,
While secrets curl in autumn leaves,
A merry song, a child's delight,
A place where joy forever weaves.

Beneath the arch of ancient trees,
The breeze carries a joyful tune,
Where stories swirl in every nook,
And magic blooms beneath the moon.

So let us wander hand in hand,
In places kissed by time's embrace,
For in these corners, laughter sings,
And every heart finds its bright place.

Fantasies Woven in Moonlight

In silver threads of moonlit dreams,
The night unveils its mystic flair,
Where wishes float on gentle beams,
And shadows dance without a care.

Beneath the canopy of stars,
A tapestry of hopes ignites,
With every sigh, a tale unfurls,
In whispers soft, through endless nights.

The owls compose a symphony,
While fireflies twinkle in delight,
As fantasies entwine with reality,
In the embrace of velvet night.

So let us dream, we'll drift away,
Through realms where hearts can freely soar,
For in this world of moonlit play,
Our spirits find what we adore.

Lights of the Forgotten Lanterns

In twilight's glow, the lanterns sway,
Their flicker tells of tales untold,
Embers of warmth in shades of gray,
A dance of light through nights of cold.

Once full of laughter, now they wait,
In silence held by time's soft hand,
Each flickering flame a whispered hope,
A promise made to understand.

Through the tangled paths of yesteryears,
Their glow recalls the heart's pure song,
Guiding lost souls with gentle cheer,
While shadows weave where they belong.

So pause a while, embrace the light,
Let fading sparks remind you to see,
For in the dark, these lanterns shine,
And lead our hearts to be set free.

Lullabies of the Dreamweaver

Close your eyes and drift away,
To lands where shadows gently play.
Where whispers weave a soft embrace,
In dreams, you find your sacred space.

Stars will twinkle, guiding light,
Through the fabric of the night.
Hold on tight, let wonder bloom,
In the heart of nighttime's room.

Silent songs the night will sing,
While the moonbeams softly cling.
Sway with peace, let worries cease,
In the arms of sweet release.

So breathe in deep, let visions flow,
In the quiet, watch time slow.
Embrace the dream, let spirits soar,
In lullabies, find evermore.

The Lighthouse of Lost Wishes

Atop the cliffs, a beacon stands,
Guiding ships with timeless hands.
With every wave, a secret shared,
In whispers soft, our hopes declared.

Wishes cast upon the sea,
Carried forth on winds so free.
Flickering lights, a path revealed,
To dreams we hold, and hearts we shield.

The tide brings tales of yesteryears,
In salt and foam, we trace our fears.
Yet steadfast shines the guiding glow,
A lighthouse where our dreams can grow.

In the night, your wish takes flight,
To the horizon, beyond our sight.
With every dawn, a chance anew,
In the light, let wishes bloom true.

Serenade for a Wandering Soul

As twilight paints the sky in gold,
A wandering heart breaks free, untold.
With every step, a story flows,
In whispered winds, the journey grows.

The stars align, a cosmic dance,
Inviting dreams, a fleeting chance.
With open arms, embrace the night,
Let fate guide you with soft delight.

Paths unknown beneath the moon,
In shadows deep, the heart attunes.
A melody of whispered sighs,
In the symphony of boundless skies.

Restless soul, chase after light,
In every corner, find your insight.
With every note, a promise unfurls,
In serenades, discover worlds.

Portals of Time and Mystery

In twilight's grip, where shadows meet,
Time unfurls its rhythmic beat.
Through swirling mist, a door ajar,
To ancient tales, both near and far.

Whispers echo of days long gone,
In the chambers where echoes spawn.
Each secret held, a story waits,
In the folds of time, behind the gates.

With every step, the past collides,
In mysteries where truth abides.
Unlock the worlds with heart and thought,
In timeless dance, the soul is caught.

So journey forth through night and gleam,
In portals vast, embrace the dream.
With open eyes, unveil the scene,
In the dance of time, forever keen.

Whirlwinds of Stardust Adventure

In the night sky, we take flight,
Chasing comets, feeling light.
Galaxies swirl, dance and play,
Whirlwinds guide us on our way.

Through black holes, we will soar,
Finding realms forevermore.
Time stands still, whispers of fate,
In this journey we create.

Stars are memories, bright and bold,
Stories of the young and old.
Adventurers of vast expanse,
With stardust dreams in every glance.

Every spark a wish untold,
In the cosmos, we are gold.
Through the darkness, we will shine,
Whirlwinds of stardust, yours and mine.

Whispers of Enchantment

In the forest, shadows weave,
With secrets only night can leave.
Mossy carpets, soft and green,
Walk with me through worlds unseen.

Moonlight dances on the stream,
Guiding all who dare to dream.
Whispers glide on gentle air,
Promises of magic there.

Twinkling lights in darkened woods,
Echo hearts from ancient broods.
Every rustle, soft and sweet,
Holds the tales of those we meet.

In this realm where wonders grow,
Nature's heart begins to glow.
In whispers, we shall forever stay,
Where enchantment lights the way.

Beyond the Glistening Veil

Beyond horizons, dreams await,
Veils of starlight, woven fate.
Hidden realms of azure skies,
Where every shadow softly lies.

Through the mists, a path appears,
Echoes of our hopes and fears.
Unlocking doors with gentle breath,
Life and love, beyond our death.

Secrets linger in the breeze,
Moments captured, hearts at ease.
In the stillness, truths unfold,
Whispers of the brave and bold.

Through the veil, we start to see,
A tapestry of what could be.
Beyond the boundaries we once knew,
Lies a world, fresh and new.

Gardens of Unseen Dreams

In the garden, petals sway,
Colors bright at break of day.
Whispers sing from blooms so rare,
Crafting visions in the air.

Roots run deep through fertile ground,
In this haven, peace is found.
Each flower holds a secret song,
In their fragrance, we belong.

Sunlight kisses every leaf,
In this realm, we find relief.
Time slows down and hopes will gleam,
Amongst the gardens of our dream.

With every step, new wonders bloom,
Casting light to chase the gloom.
Together we will weave and tend,
In gardens where our hearts can mend.

Whispers Among the Wildflowers

In fields where wildflowers sway,
Gentle whispers dance on air.
Petals share secrets, come what may,
Nature's voice, tender and rare.

Bees hum softly, a sweet tune,
Beneath the sun's warm golden gaze.
Colors blend, a vibrant boon,
In this quiet, floral maze.

The breeze carries tales so old,
Of butterflies and honeyed dreams.
Each bloom is a story told,
In the sunlight's gentle beams.

Among the blooms, the heart finds peace,
In every rustle, life's embrace.
As whispers linger, worries cease,
In wildflowers, we find our place.

The Mysterious Star Map

In the silent night's embrace,
Stars form patterns, tales to weave.
Galaxies dance in endless space,
A cosmic truth we all believe.

Each twinkle holds a distant light,
Wonders hidden, yet so near.
Constellations, guides of the night,
Whispering secrets for those who hear.

A voyager's heart can find its way,
By tracing lines of ancient lore.
Across the sky, the dreams can play,
In starry maps forevermore.

Underneath this vast expanse,
Hope ignites, ignites the heart.
With every glance, a hidden chance,
To navigate this life, depart.

The Subtle Vibrations of the Night

As dusk descends, the world grows still,
The moon casts shadows, soft and bright.
Whispers float, a gentle thrill,
In the subtle vibrations of night.

Crickets play their quiet song,
Nature's choir in tranquil air.
In this moment, we belong,
Wrapped in peace, beyond compare.

Stars glimmer with a knowing light,
Each pulse a heartbeat of the sky.
In the darkness, we find our sight,
In the quiet, we learn to fly.

With every breath, a soothing flow,
The night unveils its hidden grace.
In silence, wisdom starts to grow,
In the stillness, we find our place.

Echoes of a Timeless Tradition

Through the ages, stories bloom,
Carried on wind and whispered low.
Each tale, a thread woven in loom,
Echoes from the past gently flow.

Around the fire, hearts unite,
Voices rise in rhythmic dance.
In the shadows, flickers of light,
We share our dreams, our hopes, our chance.

With every folk song sung so clear,
The legacy of life unfolds.
In laughter shared, in every tear,
Traditions carved in heartbeats bold.

From generation to generation,
We gather to honor those before.
In joy and pain, our foundation,
Echoes guide us forevermore.

The Alchemist's Garden

In a garden where shadows play,
Gold turns to silver, night to day.
Flowers whisper ancient lore,
Secrets wrapped, forevermore.

Beneath the gnarled branches sway,
Mystic herbs in disarray.
Each petal holds an arcane dream,
Nature's magic in the seam.

With every drop of morning dew,
Alchemy feels fresh and new.
Transmute the heart, the mind, the soul,
To find the deeper, sacred whole.

In every root, a story lives,
To the curious, the garden gives.
As stars above begin to gleam,
The alchemist awakens dream.

Secrets Beneath the Ocean's Surface

Waves embrace the silent shore,
Whispers echo, tales of yore.
In the depths, where shadows creep,
Secrets guarded, oceans keep.

Coral reefs in colors bright,
Glimmer softly in the night.
Creatures dance in liquid grace,
Home to dreams, a hidden place.

Sunlight filters through the blue,
Carrying mysteries anew.
Every ripple holds a quest,
To uncover what lies rest.

Plunge into the deep unknown,
Hear the stories, depths have grown.
Bubbles rise with whispered pleas,
Secrets sung beneath the seas.

The Sound of Glittering Stones

Amidst the quiet, nature hums,
A melody of gems and drums.
Each stone resonates with a tune,
Whispers soft as the light of moon.

From sapphire blues to ruby reds,
Echoes dance where magic spreads.
Every crystal's silent song,
Tells the tales where they belong.

On rocky paths, the secrets lie,
Voices shimmer, never shy.
Listen close, the stones reveal,
Truths that time begins to heal.

In the hush between the notes,
Glimmering stones, like boats,
Sailing through the mystic night,
Guiding hearts to endless light.

The Painter's Invisible Palette

In a world where colors bleed,
A painter's heart, a vibrant seed.
Brush in hand, the canvas waits,
Imagination opens gates.

With whispers soft, he finds his hues,
Shades of hope, and morning blues.
Each stroke a story to unfold,
Mysteries within, untold.

In shades of laughter, tears, and time,
The hidden rhythms start to chime.
An invisible palette, wide and deep,
Crafts the dreams that never sleep.

With every canvas, life takes flight,
Colors dance in pure delight.
Through artistry, the soul does soar,
The painter's heart forevermore.

Secrets of the Hidden Path

In shadows deep where whispers dwell,
Silent tales the night will tell.
A winding trail, both old and new,
Beneath the stars, the secrets brew.

The trees stand guard, their leaves a canopy,
Holding memories of what used to be.
Step softly here, with heart in hand,
For hidden wonders still expand.

A flicker light, a fleeting glance,
In nature's web, we take our chance.
Echoes call from the ground so near,
Awakening dreams we long to hear.

As twilight falls, let courage guide,
Through the enchanted woods we glide.
Each turn reveals a brand new sight,
On this hidden path, we find our light.

Echoes in the Twilight Forest

In twilight's grace, the shadows play,
Where light and dark weave night and day.
A chorus calls from branches high,
As whispers drift beneath the sky.

The ancient trees, with stories rife,
Hold echoes loud, of past and life.
Footsteps soft on the mossy ground,
In nature's realm, our dreams are found.

Moonlit beams through leaves will dance,
In silence deep, we find our chance.
Each breath we take, the forest sighs,
While lingering shadows softly rise.

In stillness deep, the night unfolds,
A tapestry of tales retold.
In echo's arms, we lose our fears,
Embraced by beauty, through the years.

Dance of the Celestial Fireflies

In the velvet night, they come alive,
Tiny sparks of light that thrive.
With every flicker, they weave a song,
In a cosmic rhythm, where hearts belong.

Through fields of dreams, they skip and sway,
Dancing free, where wishes play.
A trail of glow, a fleeting sign,
Leading us closer, where stars align.

The beauty here, a sight so rare,
Illuminating dark with gentle care.
Each firefly carries a tale from afar,
A whispered wish caught in a star.

So let us dance, beneath the night,
In harmony with the celestial light.
For in their glow, our souls ignite,
A lifelong bond, in pure delight.

A Tapestry of Starlit Skies

In the vast expanse where visions lie,
The tapestry unfurls, kissed by the sky.
Each twinkling star, a story to share,
Woven gently with love and care.

The constellations, a guide for the lost,
Reminding us all of paths we crossed.
With each glimmer, hope's tender embrace,
Sparks our dreams, in quiet grace.

Beneath this dome, our hearts take flight,
In the silence of the peaceful night.
From dusk till dawn, let wonders rise,
In this beautiful, starlit prize.

So gaze above, let your spirit soar,
For the universe holds so much more.
A tapestry woven with threads of light,
In the fabric of time, we find our might.

Threads of Enchantment

In the garden where shadows play,
Whispers of magic drift and sway.
Each petal a story, softly spun,
Weaving the tales of dusk and dawn.

Moonlight threads through the leaves above,
Stitching the night with threads of love.
A tapestry bright, where dreams take flight,
We dance with stars in silver light.

Voices of wind carry secrets near,
Embroidered wishes weave through the year.
Every glance, a spark, igniting the theme,
In the heart of the night, we cherish our dream.

With every thread, a bond so tight,
Connected through darkness, into the light.
In this enchanted world, we find our way,
As threads intertwine, forever they stay.

The Symphony of the Unseen

Silent notes in the twilight air,
Play a melody beyond compare.
With every breath, the music flows,
A symphony that gently grows.

Invisible strings pull at the heart,
Crafting emotions from worlds apart.
With each heartbeat, a rhythm found,
In the silence, profound sound.

Harmony dances in shadows cast,
Echoes linger, the die is cast.
Unseen, yet felt, the magic's real,
In this symphony, we learn to heal.

Let the whispers guide us through,
In the music, we find what's true.
As shadows blend in the fading light,
We join the unseen, igniting the night.

Lights that Dance on the Horizon

A canvas of stars in the evening sky,
Where dreams take shape as they whisper by.
A flicker, a glow, a promise made,
In twilight's embrace, intentions laid.

The horizon glimmers, beckoning near,
With every light, we shed our fear.
Each spark is a wish, ignited with grace,
Dancing together in this sacred space.

As shadows surrender to the dawn,
The lights that guide us carry on.
A beacon of hope, a vision so clear,
In the heart's stillness, we draw near.

These lights shall guide through the night so long,
In their rhythm, we find our song.
With every heartbeat, we start anew,
In the dance of the horizon, we find our truth.

The Alchemy of Lost Dreams

In forgotten corners where shadows lie,
The remnants of dreams softly sigh.
A tapestry woven of wishes past,
Each thread a memory, fragile and vast.

With a whisper of hope, we blend our tears,
Transforming the pain through the years.
Alchemy brews in the heart's deep space,
Turning the loss into something of grace.

As we sift through the ashes, we find the gold,
Stories of courage that need to be told.
In the depths of despair, a spark we hold,
The alchemy of dreams, a treasure untold.

From shadows we rise, with strength reborn,
In the twilight's embrace, like a brand new dawn.
The lost dreams emerge, like phoenix in flight,
Crafting our futures with radiant light.

The Nest of Harmonious Echoes

In a grove where whispers dwell,
Soft notes of joy and peace do swell.
Branches weave a serene song,
A sanctuary where dreams belong.

Breezes carry tales anew,
In hues of green, and skies so blue.
Feathers fall like gentle rain,
In this nest, we lose our pain.

The sun shines bright through leaves so fair,
Nature's chorus fills the air.
Here, the heart finds perfect rest,
In the nest, we are our best.

As twilight paints a golden hue,
Stars emerge, a sparkling view.
In harmony, our spirits rise,
To the echoes of the skies.

Chronicles of the Moonlit Shadow

Beneath the glow of silver light,
Shadows dance, a haunting sight.
Secrets whisper on the breeze,
Tales of lovers lost at sea.

The night unfolds its velvet cloak,
Each star a word, each moonbeam spoke.
In gentle sighs, the night reveals,
The heart's deep longing, the soul's appeals.

Footprints wander on the sand,
Echoes of lives by fate's own hand.
Moonlit dreams weave through the night,
In every corner hides a light.

Chronicles penned in shadows bright,
A tapestry of love and fright.
In moonlit whispers, we confide,
The shadows hold what hearts can't hide.

Rainbows in the Mist

A gentle rain begins to fall,
Bringing colors, a vivid call.
Misty shrouds around the trees,
Promising magic on the breeze.

As sunlight breaks through silken grey,
Arches form where shadows play.
Each hue a promise, bright and bold,
A story of dreams, waiting to be told.

In the distance, a laughter rings,
Nature's joy in fluttering wings.
Footprints dance through puddles wide,
With every drop, we slide and glide.

Beneath the arcs of pure delight,
Hope is found in every light.
In the mist, our spirits flow,
Chasing rainbows, where love can grow.

The Constellation of Lost Secrets

In the night sky, stories lie,
Whispers lost as time goes by.
Stars align to weave a tale,
Of hearts that loved, but could not sail.

Fading echoes of a time once bright,
Ghosts of dreams in the pale moonlight.
Constellations map the sighs,
Of hopes and fears beneath the skies.

Every twinkling light a key,
Unlocks the past, sets memories free.
In their glow, we search for peace,
A promise made, a sweet release.

So gaze above, let visions soar,
For lost secrets will return once more.
In the cosmos, our tales still blend,
A constellation that will not end.

The Hidden Library of Stars

Beneath the ancient archway bright,
Whispers of worlds take their flight.
Pages shimmer, secrets unfold,
Galaxies captured, tales retold.

In corners dark where shadows play,
Constellations dance and sway.
Ink like twilight, stories glow,
A universe deep, a cosmic flow.

With every turn, a journey starts,
A voyage through celestial arts.
Knowledge gleaned from starlit scrolls,
Each word a key that gently tolls.

In silence held, the library waits,
For dreamers drawn to open gates.
To find the light beyond the dark,
And leave their own enduring mark.

The Enigma of Floating Islands

High above, where eagles soar,
Islands drift from shore to shore.
Mysteries dance on whispered breeze,
Clouds beneath like gentle seas.

Emerald fields and silver streams,
Dreams take root in starlit beams.
Each isle tells a tale untold,
Legends of the brave and bold.

Beneath the sun's warm, golden glow,
Nature's secrets ebb and flow.
Floating realms, a wondrous sight,
Hidden wonders, pure delight.

In every heart, an island lies,
Home to hopes that never die.
Reach for the skies, embrace the lift,
Find the gift in every rift.

Memories Etched in Silver

In twilight's embrace, a soft sigh,
Echoes of laughter drift by.
Faces blurred, yet hearts remain,
Moments of joy, shadows of pain.

Silver threads weave through the years,
Stitched with sorrows, bound by cheers.
Each memory shines, a precious gem,
A tapestry sewn, our diadem.

By fireside glow, tales are spun,
Underneath the fading sun.
Stories cherished, forever live,
In our hearts, we learn to forgive.

As twilight fades to darkened night,
Stars twinkle, a soft, guiding light.
In every heartbeat, memories flow,
A silver bond that forever will glow.

The Jester's Carnival of Curiosities

In a world where colors collide,
The jester prances, unconfined.
With laughter's twist and playful guise,
He spins tales under painted skies.

Oddities line the vibrant stalls,
Curious wonders where magic calls.
A mirror's glance reveals the strange,
In every corner, delights exchange.

Juggling dreams and fleeting time,
Notes of whimsy and sweet rhyme.
His caper draws both young and old,
In joyous moments, hearts unfold.

So step right up, don't be shy,
Join the dance, let spirits fly.
In this carnival, lose control,
Embrace the jester's wild soul.

The Flourish of Elysian Thoughts

In gardens where the sunlight weaves,
Whispers of the soul take flight.
Each petal holds a secret breeze,
Dancing in the warmth of light.

Among the trees, a gentle sigh,
Reveals the dreams we dare to share.
With every thought, we learn to fly,
In realms beyond our worldly care.

Together we shall paint the sky,
With colors drawn from hearts so pure.
In every laugh, a joyful cry,
Where hope and love will find their cure.

Through valleys deep, where shadows fade,
Our spirits meld, forever free.
In truth's embrace, we are remade,
A unity in harmony.

Hues of the Untamed Spirit

The wilderness calls out my name,
With every rustle, birds take flight.
In nature's arms, I feel no shame,
As wild as stars that grace the night.

With mountains bold, and rivers grand,
Each heartbeat echoes nature's tune.
A vibrant dance across the land,
In twilight's glow, beneath the moon.

The colors swirl, a masterpiece,
A canvas vivid, bright, and free.
In every brush, the heart finds peace,
The spirit blooms in unity.

Through uncharted paths, we find our way,
The untamed heart will never tire.
In every moment, wild and gay,
The soul ignites, a blazing fire.

Reveries on the Edge of Time

Time flows softly like a stream,
In whispered thoughts, we journey far.
Moments drift like shadows, dream,
Each tick a glimpse of who we are.

Through corridors of past delight,
We linger on the edge of fate.
In every dawn, a wish takes flight,
As futures weave, we contemplate.

With memories like stars aglow,
We chase the echoes of our dreams.
In fleeting hours, our hearts will know,
The tapestry of life it seems.

So let us dance upon this thread,
Where time and spirit intertwine.
In reveries, we're gently led,
To timeless realms where love will shine.

The Magic of Uncharted Destinies

Beyond the shores, adventures wait,
With echoes of a siren's song.
We sail on hope, we challenge fate,
Where dreams unfold and hearts belong.

Each step we take, a journey new,
With stars aligned to guide our way.
In every choice, a path we drew,
While shadows fall, we greet the day.

The magic lies in every chance,
In moments fleeting, yet so true.
As life unfolds its sacred dance,
We weave the threads of me and you.

In uncharted realms, our spirits soar,
With each new dawn, we shall explore.
Together, hand in hand, we'll find,
The destinies that love designed.

Tales of the Wandering Wanderer

Through valleys deep, the wanderer strolls,
With whispers of legends, his heart unfolds.
Each step he takes, a story untold,
In the arms of the earth, adventures behold.

Mountains high, beneath skies so vast,
With echoes of laughter, shadows are cast.
He dances with rivers, runs free and fast,
In the tapestry of time, memories last.

Stars guide his path, in the dark they shine,
As he searches for treasures, both yours and mine.
With a heart full of wonder, every road divine,
In the tales he collects, life's truths intertwine.

From dusk till dawn, the journey goes on,
With every new dawn, he greets the sun's song.
In the wanderer's heart, where dreams belong,
He finds his way home, where the brave souls throng.

The Compass of Dreams

In the quiet night, when the moon smiles bright,
A compass of dreams, guiding hearts in flight.
With whispers of hope, the stars ignite,
Showing the way, as shadows take flight.

Lost in the maze of a restless mind,
The compass spins, where fate's unconfined.
With every turn, new paths you'll find,
In the dance of the cosmos, souls aligned.

A gentle breeze carries wishes to sea,
In the heart of the dreamer, wild and free.
Through the night's embrace, let your spirit agree,
For the compass of dreams holds infinity.

Each journey begun, a story to share,
In the realm of the night, we relinquish our care.
Trust the compass, for it knows where,
The dreams we pursue are beyond compare.

Harmonies Found in Stillness

In the hush of the dawn, stillness sings,
Notes of tranquility, peace it brings.
Whispers of nature in gentle flings,
In the heart of the quiet, the soul takes wings.

Amidst the chaos, a calmness is found,
With every heartbeat, a sacred sound.
In the space between breaths, we are unbound,
In the stillness of moments, life's joys abound.

Listen closely, to the whispers of trees,
In the sigh of the wind, feel the heart's ease.
In the dance of the leaves, find your release,
In harmonies found, let your spirit please.

Nature's soft lullaby, a melody's grace,
In stillness we find our rightful place.
As echoes of silence create a space,
Where love and belonging effortlessly embrace.

The Melodies of Glimmering Nights

Beneath the starlit sky, where dreams take flight,
Whispers of magic fill the velvety night.
In the rhythm of shadows, hearts feel so light,
Dancing with stars, we relish the sight.

The moon casts its glow, a silvery beam,
In the tapestry of night, every soul can dream.
With laughter and joy, life flows like a stream,
The melodies sparkle, like diamonds that gleam.

In corners of darkness, hope softly glows,
Through the chill of the air, warmth gently flows.
As night's sweet embrace around us bestows,
The melodies linger, where love always grows.

With every heartbeat, the night sings anew,
In the embrace of the stars, we cherish the view.
In the glimmering night, our spirits break through,
For in every melody, the world feels true.

A Journey Through Fractured Memories

In shadows where the echoes fade,
I wander lost, a lonely shade.
Fragments of laughter, whispers chill,
The past, a dream that haunts me still.

Through corridors of time I fly,
Chasing glimpses, a silent sigh.
Each fleeting thought, a treasure rare,
Yet memories slip through fingers bare.

Replaying moments, like a song,
The notes are sharp, the heart feels wrong.
In the haze, I search for light,
Holding on to what's out of sight.

This journey etched in shades of gray,
A map with paths that lead astray.
Yet in the shadows, hope remains,
For every loss can yield new gains.

The Harmonious Dance of Seasons

Spring blooms forth with colors bright,
Gentle breezes, warm sunlight.
Blossoms swirl in joyful fling,
Nature sings, embracing spring.

Summer follows as days grow long,
A vibrant world, a lively song.
Golden rays and laughter clear,
Sun-kissed moments fill with cheer.

Autumn paints with hues so bold,
Leaves like fire, stories told.
Crisp air whispers of the chill,
Nature's beauty, a poignant thrill.

Winter wraps in blankets white,
Silent nights, a tranquil sight.
Frosty breath and stars that gleam,
In the stillness, we find our dreams.

The Echoing Silence of Ideas

In the chambers of the mind,
Ideas dance, though hard to find.
Whispers linger on the air,
Echoes of vision, light yet rare.

Thoughts collide like stars at night,
A cosmic clash, a spark of light.
Yet silence wraps its velvet cloak,
Each notion slowly, softly soaks.

A flash of insight, fleeting bright,
In stillness grows, takes graceful flight.
But when it fades, the quiet reigns,
Leaving behind only refrains.

Among the still, a seed is cast,
Waiting for the muse to last.
In whispered dreams and shadows deep,
The echo of ideas quietly sleep.

The Portrait of an Eternal Spring

A canvas brushed with vibrant hues,
Life awakens, in every muse.
Colors dance in joyful blend,
Nature's beauty knows no end.

Gentle rains and radiant beams,
The world unfolds in fragrant dreams.
Blossoms whisper tales untold,
In the air, warmth breaks the cold.

Butterflies flutter in delight,
As petals open, hearts take flight.
In this portrait of pure grace,
Time stands still; a sweet embrace.

Eternal spring, where spirits soar,
Life's soft essence, forevermore.
With every heartbeat, love's refrain,
In nature's arms, we live again.

Stars that Sing

In the night, they whisper soft,
Bright notes dance, a gentle loft.
Each twinkle holds a tale untold,
A melody of dreams to behold.

They weave a symphony so sweet,
A harmony where shadows meet.
Moonlight joins the starry choir,
Igniting hearts with pure desire.

Echoes drift through velvet air,
Carried on the breeze, laid bare.
In the cosmos, voices unite,
Guiding souls through endless night.

With every blink, their messages flow,
A chorus of wonder, the heavens glow.
In silence, they sing, a timeless ring,
Awake the spirit, let joy take wing.

The Canvas of Daydreams

Brush strokes of light on the horizon,
Colors blend, a soft liaison.
Imagined worlds in gentle hues,
Awakening the heart's old muse.

Each thought a petal, drifting free,
Adrift on waves of memory.
In the midst of countless schemes,
The canvas thrives with whispered dreams.

Shadows linger, dancing near,
While visions lift the weight of fear.
Creativity flows through the streams,
Painting life with vibrant themes.

In this space where hopes reside,
The soul finds peace, arms open wide.
With every splash, the heart shall sing,
In the canvas of daydreams, we take wing.

Mysteries of the Gossamer Path

A winding trail through realms unknown,
Where cobwebs weave a tale of stone.
Each step holds secrets in its grasp,
Threads of fate within its clasp.

Whispers echo in the silent air,
Voices trace in shadows, rare.
Footprints linger, then fade away,
Guiding seekers through the day.

Silken strands glimmer in the night,
Stars align with a gentle light.
Nature's story, softly spun,
In the gossamer, we're all one.

The path unfolds, a mystic dance,
Inviting souls to take a chance.
Through veils of time, we walk the line,
In the mysteries, our hearts entwine.

Journeys Through the Velvet Sky

With wings unfurled, we take to flight,
Soaring high, embraced by night.
Clouds like pillows, soft we glide,
In the velvet where dreams reside.

A tapestry of stars above,
Kisses of the moonlight love.
Galaxies swirl, a cosmic tide,
In the sky, our spirits ride.

Each journey leads to realms anew,
Horizons vast with every view.
In the silence, wonders sigh,
As we travel through the velvet sky.

Hearts open wide to what may come,
On this adventure, we've just begun.
With every leap, horizons vie,
As dreams unfold in a velvet sky.

Dawn of the Forgotten Spirits

In the hush of dawn's first light,
Whispers rise from the dark,
Spirits dance in ethereal flight,
Guiding dreams with a spark.

Ancient voices call to play,
Forgotten tales take their form,
Lost in shadows, they softly stay,
Through the mist, they will swarm.

Memories woven in twilight's thread,
Faded echoes linger still,
In every heart where they once tread,
Awakening timeless thrill.

As the sun paints skies anew,
The spirits' song softly gleams,
A dawn that blends the old and true,
Reviving long-lost dreams.

The Crystal Caverns' Lullaby

Deep within the cavern's fold,
Where crystals glimmer and glow,
A lullaby of stories told,
In whispers soft as the snow.

Stalactites drip with gentle grace,
Echoes of the ages past,
In this tranquil, sacred space,
Time itself seems to last.

Moonbeams dance on walls of stone,
Casting shadows, sweet and wide,
In this world, we are not alone,
Nature's song is our guide.

Close your eyes, let dreams take flight,
Among the gleaming shards of night,
The caverns hold all secrets dear,
A lullaby for all to hear.

Mosaic of Dreams Unraveled

In a world where colors blend,
Dreams unfold like petals bright,
Fragments dance and twist, they send,
A mosaic born from night.

Whispers of the heart awake,
Impressions of a life once known,
Each shard a choice that we can make,
Together they are beautifully sewn.

Tales of joy and sorrow weave,
Patterns formed from tears and smiles,
In every moment, we believe,
Life's tapestry spans the miles.

So let us craft with open hands,
Embrace the beauty, let it show,
In every heart, a dream that stands,
A masterpiece of love to grow.

The Symphony of Fading Colors

As twilight drapes the day in gray,
Colors fade into the night,
A symphony of hues at play,
Whispers soft, a gentle sight.

Blues and reds begin to blend,
Softly merging, drifting slow,
In the silence, colors send,
Messages of change, a flow.

With each note, a shadow falls,
Past and present, hand in hand,
In faded light, the silence calls,
A symphony we understand.

So listen close as day departs,
In the blend of dusk and dawn,
For in the fading, beauty starts,
A song that lingers, ever drawn.

The Siren's Call Beneath the Waves

In depths where shadows linger low,
A haunting voice begins to flow.
Echoes dance on ocean's breath,
Seductive song, a call to death.

With glistening scales that shimmer bright,
A beauty lost to endless night.
The waves conceal her secret lies,
A bittersweet, alluring prize.

Each sailor drawn to her sweet tune,
Meets a fate beneath the moon.
In watery graves, their spirits roam,
Forever lost, far from home.

Beware the call from ocean's edge,
For love and danger share a pledge.
The siren sings of dreams untold,
And wraps them tight in tales of old.

The Celestial Garden

In skies where stars begin to bloom,
An endless dance dispels the gloom.
Galaxies twirl in cosmic play,
In harmony, they weave the day.

Each planet stands in vibrant hue,
A tapestry of every view.
Nebulas whisper ancient prayer,
In silence held, a lover's care.

Comets streak with fiery grace,
Tracing paths through time and space.
In this garden, dreams take flight,
Suspended high in velvet night.

So gaze upon the heavens wide,
Let wonder be your faithful guide.
In cosmic blooms, our hearts will find,
The universe, both vast and kind.

Tides of Time's Embrace

With every wave that kisses sand,
Time whispers softly, hand in hand.
Moments drift like autumn leaves,
Carried forth by gentle reprieves.

The cycle flows, both swift and slow,
In ebb and flow, the feelings grow.
A dance of seconds, both lost and found,
Where memories linger, silence profound.

Each tide reveals a truth once known,
The sands of time, they gently moan.
In rhythmic pulse, we find our place,
In the vast ocean, time's embrace.

So let us cherish every hour,
As nature grants her timeless power.
For in the tide's relentless sweep,
Lie secrets that the waters keep.

Visualizing the Unseen

In shadows cast by fleeting light,
We glimpse the world from depth of sight.
A flicker here, a whisper there,
Life dances on, beyond compare.

Colors vibrate, shapes take flight,
Dreams unfold in the still of night.
Imagination paints the air,
In visions bold, our hearts laid bare.

Through veils of time, we seek to find,
The rhythm of the unseen mind.
With open eyes, we dare to see,
The magic wrapped in mystery.

In quiet moments, truth will rise,
Beyond the stars, beneath the skies.
To visualize the depths within,
Is where the journey can begin.

Fragments of an Ethereal Riddle

In twilight's haze, secrets dance,
Whispers of fate in a fleeting glance.
Echoes of worlds that softly collide,
Mysteries woven, in shadows they hide.

Glimmers of truth in a fractured light,
Clues left behind in the velvet night.
Each fragment a story, a silent song,
Guiding the lost where they all belong.

The heart beats gently, a soft refrain,
Through tangled paths of joy and pain.
Unraveling knots, they weave and entwine,
In the abyss, every soul is divine.

Through riddles unclear, we wander and roam,
Seeking our way in this vast cosmic tome.
Each question a door, each silence a key,
In fragments of life, we find what will be.

Beyond the Veil of Ordinary

Where shadows pause, and dreams unite,
Lies a realm bathed in ethereal light.
Beneath the surface of mundane sights,
The extraordinary calls on dark nights.

Veils whisper soft of secrets retained,
Tales of the lost, the loved, and the gained.
With eyes wide open, we glimpse the grace,
Hidden in moments we hardly embrace.

Every heartbeat a chance to explore,
Beyond our limits, beyond any shore.
In the dance of stars, we bow and twirl,
To the magic that sways our ordinary world.

So lift the curtain, let wonder unfold,
In the richness of life, let our spirits be bold.
Beyond the veil, with courage we tread,
In each fleeting moment, let dreams be fed.

The Wonders Hidden in Still Waters

Beneath the calm, reflections gleam,
Secrets asleep in a silent dream.
Ripples of thoughts, their whispers flow,
In tranquil depths, life's wonders grow.

Still waters guard a world unseen,
Where echoes linger, soft and serene.
In each quiet sigh, a tale silently stirs,
Of love, loss, and the heart's quiet purrs.

Through glassy surfaces, we seek the dawn,
A shimmering path to what's felt, not drawn.
The treasures await in the hush of the blue,
In every reflection, the soul finds its cue.

In stillness resides the beauty we crave,
Lessons of life that the waters gave.
So cast your gaze on the still's quiet grace,
In the wonders hidden, find your own space.

Colors of a Dreamt Reality

In hues of twilight, the world unfolds,
A canvas of dreams, where life is bold.
Colors entwined in a vibrant embrace,
Painting our stories in this sacred space.

Emerald greens and sapphire blues,
Brush strokes of laughter, shades of the muse.
Every hue tells a tale anew,
A palette of hopes, both tender and true.

In the shimmer of dawn, ochre ignites,
Fiery reds clash with soft pastel lights.
In every corner, the vivid and bright,
Reflect the beauty of our boundless flight.

So dive into dreams where colors unite,
In the tapestry woven, find your delight.
For in this vivid, dreamt reality,
Lies the essence of what we can be.

The Paradox of Impossible Paths

Footsteps dance on paths unseen,
Choices made in shadows lean.
Winding roads that twist and bend,
Guide the heart but not the end.

Echoes call from distant years,
Silent wishes, buried fears.
Every turn a secret gate,
Leading to a whispered fate.

Stars align in cosmic play,
Yet the road may fade away.
Lost in thought, the mind will roam,
Finding paths that feel like home.

In the quiet, truths are found,
On impossible ground.
Wonder lingers in the air,
As we seek, we learn to care.

Chronicles of Whispering Winds

Breezes speak of tales untold,
In the rustling leaves, words unfold.
Nature's breath carries the song,
Of all the places we belong.

Through the valleys, over hills,
Whispers weave through tranquil thrills.
Echoes dance on currents free,
Telling stories of you and me.

In the twilight, shadows blend,
Where day meets night, and pathways bend.
Each gust a message from afar,
Guiding dreams like a shining star.

Listen close, let silence reign,
In the whispers, feel the gain.
For in every gust, there lies
The essence of our endless skies.

The Secret Life of Fireflies

In twilight's glow, they burst to life,
Tiny sparks in evening strife.
Lit by secrets, they flit and roam,
Leaving trails that feel like home.

Dancing lightly, gentle grace,
Guardians of this sacred space.
Their glow a promise, bright and clear,
A fleeting wink, but ever near.

In the quiet, secrets hold,
Stories whispered, hearts unfold.
Fireflies twinkle, dreams ignite,
Painting shadows with their light.

Each night they gather, tales to share,
In their presence, magic fills the air.
A world awake beneath the stars,
Embraced by light, our hearts are ours.

Floating Dreams in a Glass Bottle

Captured wishes, sealed so tight,
Floating dreams in silver light.
Every heart a story kept,
In bottles where our secrets slept.

Glimmers dance in amber waves,
Each reflection, hope that saves.
Tides of time that ebb and flow,
Whisper dreams we yearn to know.

Message sealed with fragile care,
To the winds, we'll send our prayer.
In a world so vast and wide,
Bottled dreams are our true guide.

As the stars begin to gleam,
Let us sail upon this dream.
With each wave, we drift and glide,
Embracing life on this wild ride.

The Forgotten Orchard

In the grove where silence sleeps,
Old trees guard their secrets deep.
Fragrant blooms begin to fade,
Whispers of the past invade.

Beneath the leaves, a story lies,
Of sunlit days and moonlit skies.
Forgotten paths, the roots entwine,
Echoes lost in ancient time.

Scattered apples, bruised and sweet,
Once were feasts, now bittersweet.
Nature's canvas, painted still,
Breathes the echoes of goodwill.

But in the dusk, a light appears,
Reviving tales of bygone years.
Once again, the orchard wakes,
With every breeze, remembrance breaks.

Chronicles of the Fabled Stream

Once a trickle, now a roar,
Whispers hide on the river's floor.
Legends weave through currents wide,
The dreams of ages, side by side.

Beneath the banks, the shadows flow,
Stories buried under the glow.
Where stones listen to the tale,
Of lovers lost and ships that sail.

Rippled laughter, glistening bright,
Guides the souls through day and night.
With every splash, a secret shared,
The stream remembers, deep and prepared.

From mountain peaks to valleys low,
Each bend reveals what we must know.
Flowing onward, never still,
The chronicles of time fulfill.

Clocks that Tickle Time

Tick, tock, the seconds play,
Whirling moments slip away.
In every chime, laughter rings,
Jesting at the dance of things.

Sands of glass and winding gears,
Holding laughter, joy, and tears.
Each hour marks a story spun,
A playful race, a woven run.

In shadows cast, the minutes prance,
Inviting all to join the dance.
With every tick, a life embraced,
In the jest of time, we find our place.

So raise the hourglass high and bright,
Celebrate the fleeting light.
For in this time, both swift and slow,
The joy of living, let it flow.

Shadows of the Marvelous

In twilight's hush, dreams take flight,
Casting shapes in the dimming light.
Phantoms swirl with grace and ease,
Whispering secrets on the breeze.

Wonder weaves a subtle veil,
As shadows echo every tale.
From castles high to valleys low,
A dance of marvels, soft and slow.

Through the night, their stories meld,
Of creatures born and magic held.
In whispered tones, they gently beckon,
To realms enchanted, hearts they reckoned.

And as the dawn begins to wake,
The shadows fade, the stillness breaks.
Yet in our hearts, the marvel stays,
Sparking joy in endless ways.

Tides of Imagination

Waves of thoughts, they rise and fall,
Carrying dreams, both big and small.
Each crest a vision, each trough a chance,
To dive into worlds in a vibrant dance.

Ripples whisper secrets untold,
Of stories written, bold and gold.
In this ocean of boundless skies,
Imagination soars, as time flies by.

Sailing on currents of pure delight,
Found in the day, and deep in the night.
The tide pulls gently, a loving sway,
Guiding lost souls who wander astray.

At shore's end, where the sand meets the sea,
Lies the heart of our fantasy.
With every ebb, we rise to explore,
The tides of imagination, forever more.

Portals in the Twilight

In the dusk where shadows creep,
Magic stirs from its ancient sleep.
Glimmers of light in a mysterious hue,
Portals appear to the brave and the true.

Under the arch of the evening star,
Adventurers wander, both near and far.
Whispers of legends in the cool night air,
Calling forth seekers who dream to dare.

Each gateway leads to realms unknown,
Where fantasies flourish and wild seeds are sown.
With every step through the twilight's embrace,
We find hidden treasures, our rightful place.

As the night deepens, new paths emerge,
In the realm of the night, our spirits surge.
Together we journey into the divine,
Through portals in twilight, where wonders entwine.

The Allure of the Ethereal

In whispers soft as a gentle breeze,
The ethereal calls, inviting with ease.
A dance of spirits in shimmering light,
Enchanting the heart, igniting the night.

Veils of mist conceal ancient lore,
Each breath a promise of something more.
A fleeting glance at the world so clear,
Where dreams take flight, and doubts disappear.

Flecks of stardust in the moon's embrace,
Guide us to realms where love finds its place.
The allure unfolds, like petals in spring,
As we become one with the songs we sing.

In this tapestry woven of cosmic threads,
The ethereal beckons, where the heart treads.
Together we weave in the fabric of time,
In the allure of the ethereal, we find our rhyme.

Tales from the Fabled Woods

Deep in the woods where secrets lie,
Tales of old whisper, flutter and fly.
Among ancient trees, stories intertwine,
Magic and mystery in each twisting vine.

The deer dance lightly on paths unseen,
While fairies flit where the air is keen.
Echoes of laughter, the rustle of leaves,
Spin yarns of enchantment that no one believes.

A tapestry woven of shadow and light,
Holds the wisdom of ages in its gentle bite.
Each step a journey through myth and lore,
As we uncover treasures, and seek for more.

In the heart of the fable, adventures await,
In the whispers of trees, we discover our fate.
For in fabled woods, we're forever entwined,
In stories of wonder, our spirits aligned.

Petals of a Forgotten Universe

Petals fall from ancient trees,
Whispering tales in the breeze.
Colors fade in twilight's glow,
Echoes of secrets long ago.

Stars blink softly in the night,
Guiding dreams with gentle light.
A universe once full of grace,
Now lost in time's endless space.

Crimson skies and silver streams,
Hold the weight of lost dreams.
Each petal tells a story dear,
Of moments held and long-lost tears.

In the shadows of the past,
Memories fade but love will last.
For every petal softly sways,
A universe in a thousand ways.

The Lullaby of Starlit Fields

Night unfurls her velvet cloak,
Whispers of the wind evoke.
Crickets sing in perfect tune,
Beneath the watchful, silver moon.

Fields aglow with starlit dreams,
Glimmer softly in gentle themes.
Nature hums her sweet embrace,
A lullaby in this sacred place.

Fireflies dance, a fleeting light,
Painting stars across the night.
Each flicker brings a sweet delight,
While shadows play in soft moonlight.

So close your eyes and drift away,
To realms where night and dreams will stay.
The starlit fields, a heart's reprieve,
In whispered lullabies, believe.

Chronicles of the Moonlit Glade

In the glade where shadows play,
Moonlight weaves a silver sway.
Ancient trees hold secrets near,
Guarding tales both dark and clear.

Flickers of the night take flight,
Guided by the soft, pale light.
Gentle whispers fill the air,
Chronicles of love and care.

Footsteps echo on the ground,
In this haven, magic's found.
Every breeze a story told,
Of strength, of courage, and of gold.

So linger long in the embrace,
Of the glade's enchanted space.
For in its heart, the moonlight glows,
A tapestry of life that flows.

Secrets of the Shimmering Deep

Beneath the waves, a world unseen,
Where shadows dance and creatures glean.
Coral reefs and sapphire tide,
Hold the secrets long denied.

Fish of silver, swift and bright,
Weave between the shafts of light.
Anemones sway with grace,
In this quiet, hidden place.

Echoes of the ocean's song,
Call to those who wander long.
Every ripple tells a tale,
Of journeys wrought, in wind and sail.

So dive, dear heart, into the blue,
Where mysteries await you.
For in the deep, truths come alive,
And in that depth, our spirits thrive.

The Philosopher's Stone of Imagination

In the depths of thought, we find,
A spark of gold, a treasure blind.
Ideas dance like flickering flames,
In the mind's vast hall, with endless claims.

Crafting wonders from the air,
With dreamer's hands, we weave and dare.
Reality bends, a curious fate,
As visions bloom, we contemplate.

With every whisper, a story grows,
In twilight's grasp, the magic flows.
The philosopher's touch brings life anew,
In realms unseen, where dreams break through.

So let us grasp this stone of light,
And soar with thoughts into the night.
For in imagination's sweet embrace,
We find the world, a boundless space.

Moonbeam Reflections

Beneath the stars, the silence sings,
In moonlit dreams, our spirit wings.
Reflections dance on waters clear,
Whispers of night, we hold so dear.

Glimmers bright on shadows play,
Guiding our hearts along the way.
Each silver ray, a gentle sigh,
A tender touch from the night sky.

With every pulse, the darkness glows,
In secret paths where wonder flows.
We gather light to weave our fate,
In moonbeam hugs, we celebrate.

Let night unfold its velvet cloak,
As dreams alight and shadows choke.
In whispers soft, the stars align,
With moonlight's kiss, our souls entwine.

The Casket of Affectionate Whispers

In a casket held with gentle hands,
Lie whispers sweet of distant lands.
Soft echoes shared in twilight's glow,
A treasure chest where love will grow.

Each word a petal, soft and rare,
Blooming in hearts, an answered prayer.
The warmth of voice, a tender balm,
A soothing touch, a healing calm.

With every sigh, a promise made,
In mirrored eyes, affection displayed.
These whispers dance like autumn leaves,
In joyful hearts, true love believes.

Let's open wide this cherished trove,
Where every secret speaks of love.
In whispers soft, our souls embrace,
A timeless bond, a sacred space.

The Enchanted Compass

In the forest deep, a compass lies,
Pointing toward the magic skies.
With every turn, new paths unfold,
Adventures waiting, tales untold.

Secrets whisper through the trees,
Guiding hearts on wandering breeze.
Each direction sings a song so pure,
In the journey, we find our cure.

A twist of fate, a chance we take,
With every step, our spirits wake.
The compass spins, a dance divine,
Leading us where the stars align.

In enchanted lands, our dreams take flight,
With every dawn, we chase the light.
This compass holds the key to roam,
In the world beyond, we find our home.

Milton Keynes UK
Ingram Content Group UK Ltd.
UKHW022144111124
451073UK00007B/192